out of contr ol

Your Anger IQ

How much do you really know about dealing with anger? Take this quiz now. Then, after you read this book, take it again, compare your answers, and find out what you've learned!

1 **Your friend owes you money and hasn't paid you back. You're angry. It may be a signal that:**
a. Your friend's a jerk.
b. You feel taken advantage of.
c. You care too much about money.

2 **A coach chews you out for fouling a player on the basketball court. Your best response is to:**
a. Yell back at the coach.
b. Acknowledge your error and get on with the game.
c. Report the coach to school officials.

3 **You borrow your older sister's iPod and break it. You apologize, but she yells a nasty insult at you. How do you deal with it?**
a. Ignore her. Anger makes many people lose control.
b. Take your anger out on your younger brother.
c. Forgive her, but let her know the insults hurt. Being angry is no excuse for hurtful behavior.

4 **You have a friend who's 30 minutes late for the third time. You're steaming. You should:**
a. Yell! It's better to be honest and let your anger out.
b. Keep your emotions to yourself. It's better not to show your anger.
c. Say something like, "Look, I'm unhappy about this situation. What can we do about it?"

5 **Since your friend's parents' divorce, he seems explosively angry at times. His behavior may be a sign of:**
a. Low self-esteem.
b. Depression.
c. Relief.

Answer key:
(1) B.
(2) B.
(3) C.
(4) C.
(5) B.

Photographs © 2008: age fotostock: 89 (Assunta Del Buono), 27 bottom (Patrick Kociniak), 86 (Picture Partners); Alamy Images: 70 (Bubbles Photolibrary), 71 (Photofusion Picture Library), 63 (Ian Shaw); Corbis Images: 21 (Bettmann), 64 (Rick Gomez), 98, 99 (Jack Hollingsworth), 11, 59, 79, 92 (Image Source), 53 (JGI/Blend Images), 9 (Susan Johann), 5, 94 (Claudia Kunin), 37 (Robin Nelson/ZUMA), 58 (Pixland), 35 (Thinkstock); Getty Images: 48 (3D4Medical.com), 42 (Altrendo Images), 18, 19 (Dirk Anschutz), 24 (Duomo Photography Inc.), 75 (Brooke Fasani), 50 (Guillermo Hung), 4, 6 (Image Source), 54 (Sean Justice), 13 (Ryan McVay), cover (Jean Luc Morales), 22 (Rod Morata), 33 (Photodisc), 31 (Penny Tweedie), 73 (Yellow Dog Productions); Image Source/Pixland: 68; iStockphoto/Pascal Genest: 49; JupiterImages/BananaStock: 74; PhotoEdit: 83 (Bill Aron), 44 (Cleve Bryant), 61 (Myrleen Ferguson Cate), 39 (Tony Freeman), 27 top, 46, 47 (Michael Newman), 97 (David Young-Wolff); Photolibrary/Creatas: 66.

Cover design: Marie O'Neill
Book production: The Design Lab
CHOICES editor: Bob Hugel

Library of Congress Cataloging-in-Publication Data
DiConsiglio, John.
 Out of control : how to handle anger—yours and everyone else's /
John DiConsiglio.
   p. cm.—(Choices)
 Includes bibliographical references and index.
 ISBN-13: 978-0-531-18846-0 (lib. bdg.)   978-0-531-14771-9 (pbk.)
 ISBN-10: 0-531-18846-9 (lib. bdg.)   0-531-14771-1 (pbk.)
 1. Anger in adolescence. I. Title.
 BF724.3.A55D53 2008
 152.4'7—dc22   2007008648

©2008 Scholastic Inc.
All rights reserved. Published in 2008 by Franklin Watts, an imprint of Scholastic Inc. Published simultaneously in Canada. Printed in China. 62

SCHOLASTIC, FRANKLIN WATTS, and associated logos are trademarks and/or registered trademarks of Scholastic Inc.

9 10 R 17 16 15 14 13

How to
handle anger—
yours and
everyone else's

out of
control

John DiConsiglio

Franklin Watts

AN IMPRINT OF SCHOLASTIC INC.
NEW YORK • TORONTO • LONDON • AUCKLAND • SYDNEY
MEXICO CITY • NEW DELHI • HONG KONG
DANBURY, CONNECTICUT

all about anger

all about anger

"I HATE WHEN THEY TREAT ME LIKE A KID."

Megan's Story

Megan gets mad a lot. "I get angry when I don't understand my homework. I get angry when my parents don't let me do things I really want to do. Sometimes all my friends will be going somewhere like to a party or to the mall, and they won't let me go. I hate when they treat me like a kid."

Inside Anger

Megan has developed some constructive ways to deal with anger. Often, she puts on music, flips through a magazine, or calls a friend. And before long, whatever made her mad seems to slip away. "I guess the best thing is to do something that takes your mind off it," she says.

Megan's story probably sounds familiar. Everyone gets mad. And everyone deals with their anger in different ways. Some kids write in journals. Some exercise. Others listen to music, watch TV, or just talk with a friend. There are as many ways of blowing off steam as there are reasons for getting hot in the first place.

"In some ways, anger is the most basic and, at the same time, most complicated emotion," says Dr. Daniel L. Davis, a psychologist and expert on teen anger issues. "A lot of people don't know much about it."

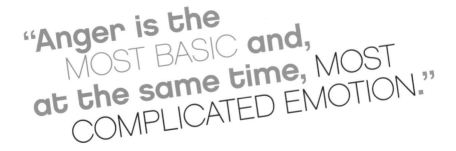

"Anger is the MOST BASIC and, at the same time, MOST COMPLICATED EMOTION."

Anything can trigger our anger. It comes over us when we think we've been hurt or mistreated. Sometimes we feel it when there's an obstacle blocking us from attaining a goal.

Temper Tally

Some experts say the average person gets angry about **once a day**—and annoyed or irritated about **3 times a day**.

Other anger experts say that getting angry **15 times a day** is more realistic.

There is a physical part to anger—it makes our bodies feel a certain way. There are psychological explanations for anger, and there are social factors as well.

Often, the ways we express anger have to do with what we were taught or what we saw in our own homes. Anger is an emotion, not a behavior. While everyone feels anger, not everyone knows how to handle their anger, and that can lead to frightening situations. Some people are so quick-tempered that it's scary to be around them. Others get into fistfights. For some people, anger can lead to taking dangerous risks like abusing drugs and alcohol.

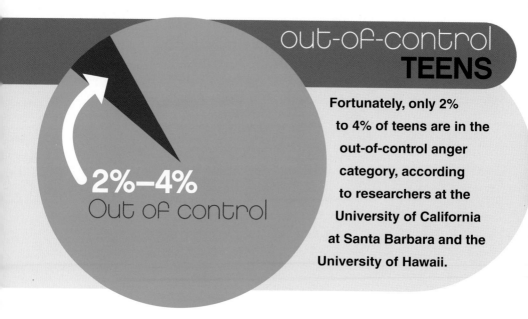

out-of-control
TEENS

2%–4%
Out of control

Fortunately, only 2% to 4% of teens are in the out-of-control anger category, according to researchers at the University of California at Santa Barbara and the University of Hawaii.

But there's a positive side to anger, too. It can show us that a problem exists. It can motivate us to fix things that aren't working in our lives. It can spur us to face problems and deal with them. And it can force people to take action when struggling with traumatic issues like abuse or **depression**.

No matter what your anger looks like, anger is a common and unavoidable emotion—even though it has real physical and psychological consequences. Like it or not, you're going to get angry just about every day. Getting angry is easy. The tricky part is learning to recognize where your anger is coming from and knowing how to deal with it.

What Really Makes Us Mad?

Paul, a 16-year-old basketball star from Wisconsin, gets angry when he's frustrated, whether it's by a referee's bad call or a bad grade on a test. Amy, a 15-year-old from Georgia, gets frustrated when she feels ignored. "Sometimes I think no one is listening to me," she says. "That gets me depressed."

ANGER can hide these emotions → grief fear sadness longing

N'Chelle, a 16-year-old from Washington, D.C., gets riled when people treat her badly. "I don't let kids walk all over me," she says. "If you do something to me, I'm going to turn around and give it right back to you." That tactic hasn't worked, though. N'Chelle was suspended last year for punching a girl in the nose.

Robert, a soft-spoken 17-year-old from South Carolina, tries not to get angry at all. But he admits that the pressures of teen life wear on him sometimes. "When you're my age, you're dealing with so much— getting good grades, getting into a college, just

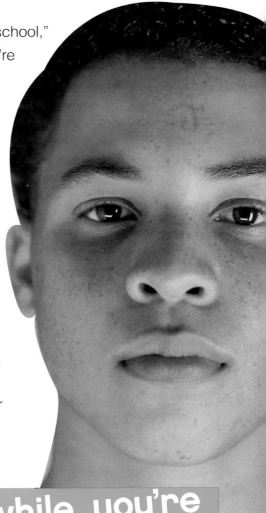

dealing with being in high school," he says. "After a while, you're like, can't people just give me a break?"

For teens, there are all sorts of circumstances in which you just can't help getting angry. Usually your anger comes from feeling you have been treated badly. Sometimes it comes from something standing in your way, keeping you from getting what you want. Other times, anger can be a reaction to feeling frustrated, left out, or even confused.

"After a while, you're like, can't people just give me a break?"

Maybe a rule at home is setting you off—like a curfew or a grounding or your mom yelling at you to clean up your room before you go out. Maybe it's a fight with a friend. Or learning you didn't get a part in the school play.

Anger also can come out of grief. The loss of a friend or relative or even a pet can make you feel both sad and mad. Stress at school or home is a common source of anger, too.

One more hidden source of anger is the belief that you have to be perfect. Being perfect is a pretty high bar—an impossibly high one. And people naturally get angry when they fail at things they think they can achieve. The problem with **perfectionism** is that you think you can achieve the impossible, which leaves you feeling angry a whole lot. If this sounds like you, you may not need to work on your anger as much as you need to work on not being perfect. Or think about that another way: You need to work on letting yourself be human. Humans make mistakes.

Be warned: spotting the source of your anger isn't as easy as it sounds. Anger can be tricky. You may yell at someone but actually be angry at someone else. That's called **displaced anger**. It's when we redirect our anger at someone or something other than what's really making us angry.

Imagine you are angry at a teacher for giving you a bad grade. But instead of telling the teacher how you feel, you yell at your little brother when you get home. It looks like you are mad at your brother. But you're *really* ticked off at your teacher!

Anger can be TRICKY.

MAD attack!

Parents bugging you? School getting you down? We asked teens to tell us what gets them angry.

Paul

I get angry when people won't listen to me. It makes me angry when I'm trying to do something and other people are getting in my way.

Amy

I get really angry when my little brother and sister are bugging me. My brother will do things like take my CDs without asking. I hate that! I hate when my parents take my brother and sister's side all the time just because they are younger.

N'Chelle

Sometimes my friends make me really angry. They are supposed to be my friends and stick up for me. But a lot of times, it feels like they only care about themselves. I get mad when people get in my face. It makes me mad when people are jerks and lie about something you didn't do.

Robert

Stupid little things get me mad, like when I can't find where I put things. It makes me feel stupid because it isn't really worth getting mad about. Then when something big happens—like when you get into a fight with your parents—you think about how dumb you must have seemed getting mad over small things.

Do Teens Get Angrier Than Adults?

Some experts believe that teens get angrier than adults. Part of this is due to the changes your body goes through during adolescence. All those hormones coursing through you can cause mood swings and confused emotions.

Young people are just learning how to express lots of different emotions. According to Dr. Bernard Golden, a psychologist, teens feel all emotions more strongly than adults. "Teen are much quicker to act on emotion without thinking," Golden says. "They are just beginning to learn how to deal with their anger."

You can thank your brain chemistry for that. Experts know that your brain is growing into your early twenties. And the last part of the brain to reach maturity is the section that governs judgment and decision making—the exact skills you need to

view your emotions with understanding and to react thoughtfully!

Teenagers face tough issues during adolescence. You're under a lot of stress. With your energy going toward school, your friends, and maybe trying to get into a college, you may be feeling the heat. You may be dealing with questions about your identity. Or maybe you're separating from your parents. That makes matters tense as you and your folks both deal with your need for independence. Your frustration—and theirs—can easily shift into anger.

"Kids naturally feel angry when they don't think people listen to them," says Edmund Benson, founder of the ARISE Foundation, which offers anger management programs to young people. "The more someone feels ignored or that their opinion doesn't matter, the angrier they are going to get. For a lot of teenagers, those feelings are common."

THE
UPSIDE
of anger

Anger isn't always bad for you. Believe it or not, anger can motivate you to do great things.

History is filled with examples of people who were motivated to right wrongs—once they got angry enough to act! Dedicated crusaders for moral causes—like Dr. Martin Luther King Jr.'s drive for civil rights or Mahatma Gandhi's work for Indian independence—said anger gave them the strength to persevere. After her daughter was killed by a drunk driver, Candy Lightner got so angry she organized MADD (Mothers Against Drunk Driving) to get drunk drivers off the road.

Anger has helped people leave bad situations, such as abuse at home. When a long-suffering victim of abuse finally reaches the anger boiling point, the emotion can motivate that person to leave a bad relationship.

In your own life, anger might motivate you to study harder for a test. "You might be fed up with getting Cs and think, 'Darn it, I'm going to change all this,'" Golden says. Being angry can make you feel like you have control of a situation, rather than letting it control you.

enraged

enraged

"I WAS FURIOUS."

Paul's Story

It was crunch time in Paul's basketball game. So when his high school coach called a time-out with just a few seconds left, Paul knew what was coming. Or at least he thought he knew.

"I was sure he was going to say, 'Get the ball to Paul,'" says the 16-year-old star player from Milwaukee. "I thought I was going to take the game-winning shot."

Instead, the coach called a new play. Someone else would take the shot. "Paul," the coach said, "you're on the bench."

"I was furious," Paul says. "I couldn't figure out why he was benching me." But Paul was being benched precisely because he was so furious. Throughout the game, he yelled at his teammates. He threw a water bottle and kicked the chairs on the sideline. And it wasn't the first time.

When Anger Turns into Rage

Paul regularly screamed at the other players. He stomped his feet on the court. When a foul was called on him for pushing an opposing player, he was so irate that his coach feared he might hit somebody. Finally, the coach made a decision. Paul was suspended from the basketball team until he got help. Paul was outraged. But everyone from his teachers to his coach to his parents could see that his anger was verging on **rage**.

Everyone has lost control of their temper at some point. It can lead to embarrassing incidents that you're sorry for later, like saying mean things to a friend.

Uncontrolled anger can be harmful. It's possible that it can contribute to the development of migraine headaches, heart disease, and cancer. It can cause people to lose their friends and their relationships. And it can make people feel uncomfortable with themselves and with others.

UNCONTROLLED **ANGER** can be harmful.

At its worst, out-of-control anger can lead to violent outbursts. It might provoke you to throw a plate, kick a door, or even punch a hole in the wall. And it can be even more extreme. Rage has led people to hurt themselves—and others.

Anger Versus Rage

Everyone gets angry. But for some, the needle pushes past anger and explodes into rage. When anger grows out of control, it becomes more than a healthy emotion or even a minor annoyance. It becomes a fierce and frightening temper explosion. It becomes rage. Rage has many consequences. It **alienates** friends and family. It also can contribute to the development of some health problems.

Most experts say a good way to tell if you have rage issues is to look at the frequency of your anger and its intensity. "Are you getting angry several times a day?" asks Dr. Bernard Golden. "How long do you hold on to [your anger]? A half hour? Or are you holding on to it for hours and hours—if not days?"

The intensity of your anger can also signal whether it has gone too far. If you become violent or abusive, your anger has turned into rage. You might black out and forget what you did. Or your actions may later seem to you like gross overreactions. In all these cases, your anger has become unmanageable.

Other people may notice anger problems before you do. Ask yourself if your friends have started avoiding you. "They often see it before you do," Golden notes.

WARNING SIGNS

Q: How do I know if my anger is out of control?

A: Here are some warning signs. If you see these in yourself or a friend on a frequent basis, you may be dealing with rage issues.

You get angry at everything that inconveniences you, annoys you, or gets in the way of what you want to do.

You act out aggressively or violently, by yelling, ranting, hitting, shoving, or plotting revenge.

Your angry feelings consume you long after the event that made you mad has passed.

Things that never used to make you angry are suddenly **major issues in your life** and send you into a rant. Maybe you explode when somebody gets a higher grade than you. Or you curse and scream when a kid takes too long in the lunch line.

You find yourself **doing self-destructive things** to cope with your angry feelings, like driving recklessly, fighting, abusing drugs and alcohol, or acting out sexually.

Know Your Triggers

What sets you off? Your little brother? Your homework? Or is it when your parents check up on you and treat you like, well, a kid?

All the things that make you angry—from the minor annoyances like someone stepping on your new sneakers to major factors like failing a test or your girlfriend or boyfriend dumping you—are called **triggers**. They light your fuse. And while anger is a normal—even helpful—emotion, it can be a problem if you don't recognize it or if it always sends you into a rage.

The first step in gaining control over your emotions is to be aware of when and why you are feeling anger. It helps if you recognize your body's reactions to anger, like stomach pain, headaches, or a flushed feeling in your face. And it's important to know your triggers. Stop to think about what situations make you lose control. Maybe a friend who brags makes you feel stupid. Or a teacher who doesn't call on you makes you feel unimportant.

TRIGGER TEST

If you know your triggers, you'll know when to watch out for anger. Here are some common triggers. To see how they affect you, number them from 1 (triggering a mild reaction) to 5 (bringing on a rage).

After you've rated each one, look over your numbers to see what your triggers really are. Keep an eye out for those situations.

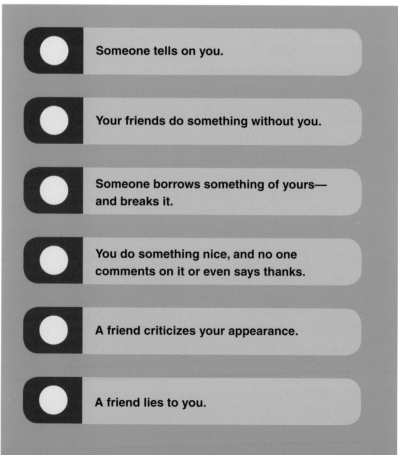

Someone tells on you.

Your friends do something without you.

Someone borrows something of yours—and breaks it.

You do something nice, and no one comments on it or even says thanks.

A friend criticizes your appearance.

A friend lies to you.

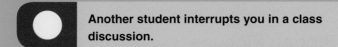
Another student interrupts you in a class discussion.

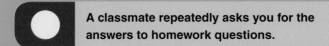
A classmate repeatedly asks you for the answers to homework questions.

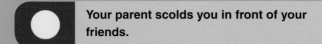
Another student brags about her grades.

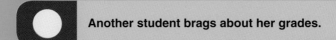
Your parent scolds you in front of your friends.

The Bigger Picture

While all of us feel angry at some point, severe anger attacks—out-of-control rage, frequent outbursts, and gross overreactions to minor annoyances—are more frequent among people with some form of emotional problems.

Anger is a common symptom of depression. In fact, many experts define depression as anger turned inward. Studies have shown that people suffering from depression are about 50 percent more likely to have frequent anger attacks than others.

Anger is also common among people with **bipolar disorder**. That's a type of depression in which people experience dramatic mood swings, from overly energetic to hopelessly sad. During their manic—or energetic—phases, many people with bipolar disorder suffer from extreme irritability and anger.

50%

Studies have shown that people suffering from depression are about 50% more likely to have frequent anger attacks than others.

"One of the reasons that it's so important to recognize when you have an anger problem is because it can easily be masking a serious [emotional problem]," says Dr. Daniel L. Davis. "Sometimes anger is a sign that there is something else very serious going on."

For others, anger is a signal that something terrible is going on in their lives, such as abuse. Someone who is irritable or frequently angry may be hiding from or reacting to an extreme situation at home. Victims of sexual or physical abuse are often mistrustful of others, Davis says. Instead of discussing their problems, they may react with anger. "Anger is never as clear as it first seems," he says. "We often think someone is being a jerk. But if you scratch the surface, there's almost always something happening underneath."

Fight Club!

For too many kids, the way to vent their anger is fighting.

N'Chelle spent much of her junior year in her high school principal's office. She wasn't there for bad grades or cutting class; she was there for fighting.

Someone was always in N'Chelle's face. Or someone was spreading lies about her. Or someone was calling her names. And when N'Chelle felt threatened, when she felt insulted or disrespected, she didn't back down. She fought back.

But instead of standing up for herself or telling people to leave her alone, N'Chelle got into fights. The last straw was when she broke a girl's nose. That's when she was suspended. If she wanted to return, school officials told her, she'd have to enter a teen anger management program.

Her reaction? You guessed it. "I was mad," she says. "I felt like hitting somebody."

Months later, N'Chelle came to understand that she usually resorted to violence when she got angry. And she's not the only teen with this response.

Fighting is a very common expression of teen anger. You see it in schools every day. According to the National Youth Violence Prevention Resource Center, more than 33 percent of high school students have been in a physical fight. About 14 percent have fought on school property. And 11 percent of those who fought were hurt badly enough to need medical treatment.

"It wouldn't be too strong to say that teen fighting is an epidemic," Friendler says.

Although there are any number of reasons that teens resort to fistfights, most experts agree that teens who continually get into fights aren't able to talk about the things that bother them. "We usually see them come from households where people didn't talk about what they are feeling,"

"It wouldn't be too strong to say that teen fighting is an epidemic."

Golden says. "As a result, as these kids get older, they don't have the language they need to resolve conflicts. The only way they know how to resolve them is with their fists."

Edmund Benson, of the ARISE Foundation, works primarily with high-risk teens, many of whom have been jailed for violent crimes. To him, the secret to dealing with teen violence is deceptively simple. "We teach instructors to listen to these kids," Benson says. "Their biggest frustration is that they haven't been listened to. When someone sits down and talks to them—without making a judgment or getting mad at them—you'd be surprised at how quickly their anger eases."

WHY teens FIGHT

Here's how junior and senior high school students around the nation responded when they were asked to identify all the causes of the most recent fights they'd witnessed.

Source: Harvard-MetLife

54% Someone insulted someone else or treated them disrespectfully.

44% There was an ongoing feud or disagreement.

42% Someone was hit, pushed, shoved, or bumped.

40% Someone spread rumors or said things about someone else.

39% Someone could not control his or her anger.

34% Other people were watching or encouraging the fight.

26% Someone who likes to fight a lot was involved.

21% Someone didn't want to look like a loser.

19% There was an argument over a boyfriend or girlfriend.

17% Someone wanted to earn or keep a reputation.

WHO'S fighting?

BOYS **FIGHT MORE THAN** GIRLS

About 44% of male high school students versus 27% of female high school students said they had been in a fight in the past year.

Source: Centers for Disease Control and Prevention

YOUNGER **TEENS FIGHT MORE THAN** OLDER **TEENS**

More than 40% of ninth graders said they had been in a fight in the past year, in contrast to 30% of twelfth graders.

Source: Centers for Disease Control and Prevention

TEENS WHO USE ALCOHOL AND DRUGS ARE MUCH MORE LIKELY TO DO HARM

People who fight when they are drunk or high are much more likely to use weapons and cause serious injuries. This includes teens using marijuana, cocaine, and anabolic steroids. More than 60% were seriously injured (had broken bones, loss of consciousness, knife or gunshot wounds), and more than half used weapons. When alcohol and drugs were not involved, only 18% of the fights involved serious injuries or weapon use.

Source: *Archives of Pediatrics and Adolescent Medicine*

ANGER
Leads to the
ER

About **10%** of emergency room visits could be avoided if people didn't take action when they were angry. At three ERs in Missouri, injury patients who felt "irritable" before their incidents were 30% more likely to get hurt, while "hostile" people had double the injury risk.

Source: Annals of Family Medicine

DRUGS, ALCOHOL, and anger

Do people abuse drugs because they have anger issues? Or do anger problems lead to drug abuse?

The answer is: both.

People who abuse drugs are less likely to have control over their behavior, particularly their anger. "In that state," says psychologist Dr. Daniel L. Davis, "their decision making is impaired. They are very likely to express their anger in ways that will get them in trouble."

On the other hand, kids who already struggle with anger issues may seek out drugs and alcohol to hide their anger from others or to block their pain. "Some kids use [drugs and alcohol] to self-medicate their feelings of anger," says Dr. Bernard Golden.

the science
of anger

the science of anger

"EVEN YOUR EYES FEEL HOT"

N'Chelle's Anger

A girl at school accused N'Chelle, a 16-year-old from Washington, D.C., of stealing from her locker. N'Chelle denied it, but the girl didn't back down. She yelled at N'Chelle in the hallway and called her a liar.

That's when the changes started. N'Chelle began to breathe faster. Her heart pounded in her chest. She even started sweating a little. Before long, she clenched her fist.

"When you get that way, your whole body feels like it's in a knot," N'Chelle says. "You feel all tight in your chest. And even your eyes feel hot."

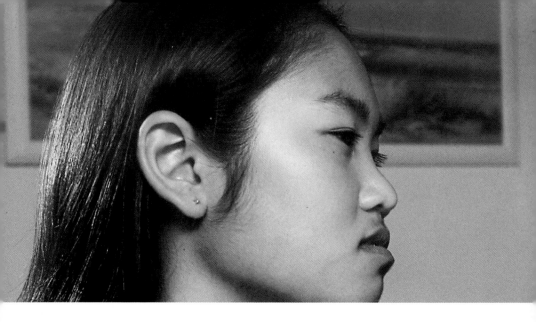

You know the feeling. And you know the phrases that describe it. Your blood is boiling. You're seeing red. You're losing your cool.

Anger is a powerful emotion—so powerful that it causes changes in your body and your brain. When you get angry, your brain rapidly fires off chemicals, sending signals throughout your body. Your temperature rises, your jaw tightens, your muscles tense. You may even shake.

In this chapter, we'll take a deeper look at exactly what goes on in your body and your brain when you get angry. We'll look at how out-of-control anger affects your health. And we'll figure out why some people stay cool—while others are hotheads.

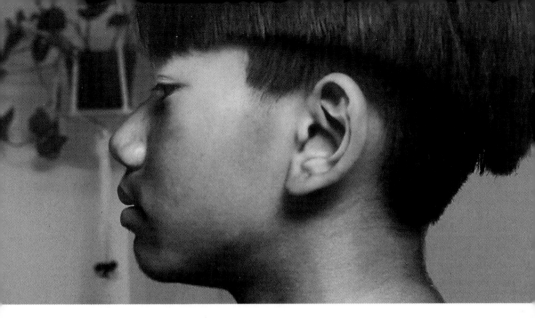

Anger and Your Body

As your temper flares, your body goes through major changes.

N'Chelle clenched her fist and narrowed her eyes. She was getting ready for a fight. She was responding to a threat—another girl calling her a thief and a liar. And inside, her body was responding to her anger.

What happens inside your body when you get angry? Let's start deep within your brain. That's where we'll find two almond-shaped structures called the **amygdala**. That's basically where anger—and many of your other emotions—begins.

AMYGDALA

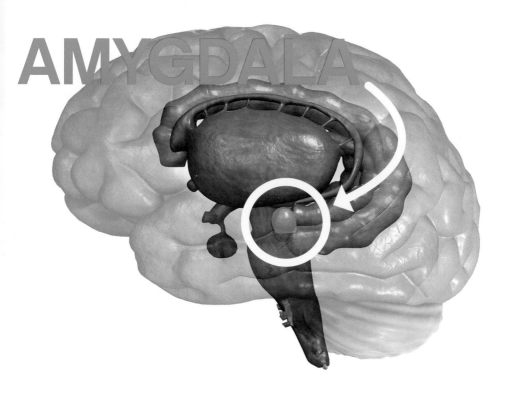

The amygdala is the part of the brain responsible for identifying threats—whether someone is attacking you physically or emotionally. The amygdala is so good at warning you about threats that it makes you react before the **cortex**— the part of the brain responsible for rational thought—can figure out whether the threat is real or you're overreacting. In other words, our brains are wired to fight first and ask questions later.

Inside your brain, chemicals known as **catecholamines** are released, causing you to experience a burst of energy that can last several minutes. At the same time, your heart rate accelerates, your blood pressure rises, and your breathing grows faster. Your face may flush as more blood flows into your limbs. Your attention narrows and becomes locked on the target of your anger. Soon you can pay attention to nothing else. Quickly, more brain chemicals and hormones are released, including **adrenaline**, which makes you more alert and ready for action. Now you're itching for a fight.

Here's the good news: This is the precise moment when the reasoning center of your brain steps in. Just behind your forehead is a part of your brain called the **prefrontal cortex**. It keeps your emotions in check and handles judgment. Getting control over your anger means learning ways to help your prefrontal cortex get the upper hand over your amygdala.

Anger also has a cooldown phase. As time goes by, we relax and return to our normal state, usually when the target of our anger has left or we no longer feel threatened. But it's not easy to relax from an angry state. The adrenaline surge can keep us angry for hours, maybe even days. During this phase, our anger threshold is lower. That means we're more likely to get angry over minor irritations that normally wouldn't bother us.

FIGHT or Flight?

Adrenaline is one of the main hormones responsible for what is called the **fight-or-flight response**. That's the automatic reaction your body has to a threat. It's a signal that gets your body ready to either face the threat head-on—or run away from it.

When you feel threatened, either physically or emotionally, your brain stimulates your adrenal glands, located above each of your kidneys. The glands flood your body with adrenaline, a chemical that signals your body to increase blood sugar, which makes energy. That helps you handle an emergency. And it fuels your reactions, including your emotions. As your energy rises and you breathe faster, your heart responds by pumping your blood more quickly. As your temperature rises, your body begins to perspire to cool itself down. When the adrenaline hits a high point, your body kicks into fight-or-flight mode and you're already feeling intense emotion.

WHY?

Why Am I Angry?

We know why our bodies react to anger. But what's happening in our minds? Anger is part biological, and it's also part psychological. That means the answer to why we get angry doesn't stop with the way our bodies work. It also has a lot to do with our minds.

Anger is with us from birth to old age. There is scientific evidence that some children are born with irritable, sensitive, and easily angered natures. But no one is born with a chronic anger problem. Our anger styles are learned. And we can learn to manage them—if we figure out what's behind them.

Where does your anger style come from? The way you react to anger is likely a result of your family background and role models. To a great extent, the way people handle anger depends on how they have been taught to handle their own feelings—and what they saw at home.

Does your family talk about emotions?

In many families, people don't talk about their feelings. Instead, they quickly act them out. In families like this, anger issues are likely to develop. Imagine parents or guardians who lash out when a kid brings home a poor report card. Rather than saying, "I'm disappointed, and I know you can do better," they yell all night about everything from a kid's elbows on the dinner table to his messy room.

A child from that family would have little experience discussing his feelings. Instead, his first reaction would be to overreact. "Kids who come from family backgrounds that are chaotic and aren't very good at emotional communication are at risk of anger problems," says Dr. Daniel L. Davis.

How does your family react to your anger?

When you were younger, how did adults around you handle your angry outbursts and temper tantrums? Did they clearly explain what kind of behavior they expected from you?

Too often, adults are uncomfortable with conflict and anger—and they pass that feeling on to their kids. The child begins to feel that all anger is bad. Or she feels so ashamed of being angry that she learns to swallow it up. "Children who have been taught that it's wrong to be angry will tend to suppress their anger," says Dr. Louise Friendler. But eventually that anger will resurface.

How do your parents handle their own anger?

The way your parents or guardians handle their anger can influence how you deal with your own. Some people learn to be angry in childhood by copying the behavior of angry people around them. For instance, children growing up in a household where one parent yells at and criticizes the other learn that behavior. As they grow up, they often show the same harsh behavior in their own relationships.

Dr. Bernard Golden refers to what he calls the "spilled milk" scenario. Think about what you were told when you spilled milk at the kitchen table. "One parent might say, 'Gee you had an accident. I'll help you with that. Try to be careful next time,'" Golden says. "Another parent might say, 'You clumsy, stupid idiot! Everything you do is wrong!'"

One child learns to work through mistakes. The other is given "a mass devaluing" and feels worthless, Golden says. "That's the behavior they model and copy and will pass on through their life."

Is Anger INHERITED?

The American Psychological Association does not accept a genetic link to anger. But some scientists believe that at least some of our anger behaviors are inherited.

Remember: anger happens when chemicals are released in our brain in response to something we perceive as a threat. These chemicals are made from instructions found in our genes. Many experts believe that the degree to which these chemicals produce anger signs may be related to those genes. In theory, one person could get angry more easily than another due to their genetic makeup.

Still, genetics is just one possible factor. Even if your anger style is inherited to some degree, it also relies heavily on your environment and the way you react to it.

Warning: Anger Is Bad for Your Health

Anger can be a major health hazard. Paul's shouting gives him headaches. Amy's pent-up anger makes her stomach hurt. N'Chelle's feelings of rage make it hard for her to fall asleep some nights.

These are just some of the physical effects that anger has on your body. Intense anger isn't good for you. In the short run, rampant anger can lead to stomachaches, diarrhea, or headaches. In the long run, doctors warn that anger is a factor in heart disease, arthritis, and cancer.

- Several studies show that chronic anger raises your risk of developing various deadly forms of heart disease to as much as five times the normal rate.
- Some studies have shown that men who have poor anger management skills are more likely to suffer heart attacks at early ages. At Duke University Medical Center, researchers found that people who were frequently angry are 50 percent more likely to have blocked coronary arteries.

- Your anger is also the most accurate predictor of whether you'll develop heart disease—even more than your cholesterol level, alcohol use, cigarette smoking, or weight.
- These health problems can start in childhood. One University of Pittsburgh study followed 134 children with anger issues. It found that the angrier kids are, the more likely they are to develop health problems such as heart disease, high blood pressure, and obesity when they're older.

So how does anger affect our health? One explanation is that hostility causes stress. Some people can handle stress with little effect on their bodies. Others have bad physical reactions to stress. As a reaction to stress, the body produces hormones that cause your heart to beat more strongly and your blood pressure to rise. When this happens a lot, there can be damage to coronary arteries around your heart. The stress hormones cause fat to be released into the bloodstream, which raises cholesterol levels and may block arteries.

Gender Wars

For years, many scientists assumed that only boys expressed their anger through physical aggression.

Recent studies have found that girls can be just as physically aggressive as boys, however. "It doesn't necessarily mean girls are more angry, just that they have started to express it more physically," Dr. Davis says.

In the past, Davis says, researchers typically saw girls express their anger socially, for instance, in dominating relationships or gossiping. Boys tended to be more physical, shouting or getting into fights.

But that's changed. Why have girls grown more aggressive in the last few years? No one's sure. It may be an unfortunate by-product of something positive: girls feeling more confident about standing up for themselves. Or it could be caused by increased peer pressure on teens. Girls' aggression seems to rise in middle school, when they can often feel excluded from social cliques. Experts also point to a rise in depression among teenage girls.

"We have to redefine what aggression looks like in girls," Davis says. "We obviously haven't been reaching girls like we should."

WHY have girls grown more aggressive in the last few years? **NO ONE'S SURE.**

"We have to redefine what aggression looks like in girls."

ANGER SIGNS

Be on the lookout for these physical and emotional warning signs. If you experience them frequently, you may have an anger problem.

PHYSICAL Signs of Anger

- Clenching your jaw or grinding your teeth
- Headache
- Stomachache
- Rapid heart rate
- Sweating, especially your palms
- Feeling hot in the neck and face
- Shaking or trembling
- Dizziness
- Rubbing your head
- Cupping your fist with your other hand
- Pacing

EMOTIONAL Signs of Anger

- Feeling like you want to get away from everything
- Feeling irritated
- Being sad or depressed
- Feeling guilty
- Being resentful
- Feeling anxious
- Wanting to strike out verbally or physically
- Getting sarcastic
- Losing your sense of humor
- Acting in an abusive or abrasive manner
- Raising your voice
- Yelling, screaming, or crying

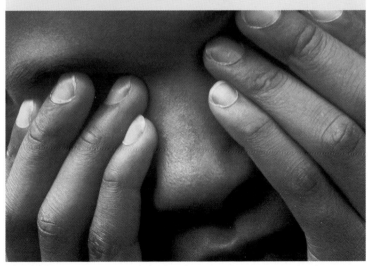

taming
your
temper

taming your temper

"IT WAS LIKE I WAS ABLE TO TAKE A DEEP BREATH."

Paul Finds Help

These days, when Paul feels angry, he grabs his sneakers and goes for a run. The angrier he gets, the farther he runs. "Sometimes," he laughs, "I go for miles." As his heart pumps and his muscles strain, Paul feels his anger easing. By the end of his run, he can barely remember why he was so mad in the first place.

For Paul, understanding anger didn't come naturally. He needed help. His parents took him to a psychiatrist, who recommended that Paul take time off from the basketball team. At first, Paul's father resisted the idea. Basketball, he reasoned, was the only thing that made Paul feel good about himself. The psychiatrist said that was the exact reason why he should take a break from it. Too much of his self-esteem was wrapped up in basketball. "Once I got away from it," Paul says, "I kind of relaxed. It was like I was able to take a deep breath and not worry about it anymore."

Do You Control Your Anger?
Or Does It Control You?

Because anger can be so powerful, managing it is often challenging. But anger isn't something we should ignore or avoid. In fact, as the teens in this book have shown, when we get to know our anger—what triggers it, how we react to it—we can learn how to manage it. It takes plenty of self-awareness and self-control to manage angry feelings. And these skills take time to develop.

In this chapter, we'll look at different ways to manage your anger—from exercise to role-playing to simply avoiding what makes you mad. Different tactics work for different kids. And while some people can change their behavior by themselves, others, like Paul, find help anywhere they can get it.

"At first, it's weird telling someone, 'Yeah, I have an anger problem,'" Paul says. "But once you say it, you feel like you have so much off your chest. I didn't even know I was carrying that around with me."

"At first, it's weird telling someone, 'Yeah, I have an anger problem.' But once you say it, you feel like you have so much off your chest. I didn't even know I was carrying that around with me."

What Doesn't Work?

Which is healthier: keeping your anger buried inside you, or letting your rage explode for the whole world to see? Experts have a pretty clear message when it comes to that debate: both can be destructive. And both have consequences—to yourself, to your health, and to the people around you.

"Anger is natural. It's best to deal with it realistically. You can never eliminate it. But you can't let it control you either," Dr. Daniel L. Davis says. Confronting anger doesn't mean expressing every angry thought you have, he adds. But dealing with it reasonably doesn't mean keeping it all inside.

"Anger is natural. It's best to deal with it realistically."

KEEPING
IT IN

Keeping anger bottled inside usually just makes it worse. When people do it for a long period of time, there can be serious results, including:

- **Hurting themselves** emotionally and physically. Instead of pointing their anger at what's really making them mad, people might point it at themselves—and feel worthless. Those feelings can be so painful that they hurt themselves to stop them.

- **Withdrawing from life.** Being angry can make it hard to be around other people. Someone who is angry might pull away from friends or family members and prefer to be alone all the time.

- **Taking risks.** People with a lot of rage inside them can sometimes do crazy, dangerous things. They might try to start fights they have no hope of winning or drive recklessly or go places that aren't safe.

- **Developing a negative attitude.** Keeping all that anger bottled up inside can color a person's picture of the whole world, causing what Davis calls "awful-izing." That's when people find themselves always expecting the worst to happen or seeing the worst in people.

- **Having trouble making and keeping friends.** Being sullen and angry can turn people off. In some ways, teens who direct their anger inward may be trying to ward off friends because they don't feel like they deserve them.

- **Developing physical pain or illnesses.** Migraines, stomachaches, diarrhea, trouble sleeping or eating—people can develop all of these by suppressing their anger.

- **Using alcohol or drugs.** Many people think that numbing themselves with alcohol or drugs will quell the anger inside them. This never works. Using drugs and alcohol is just a way to avoid the problem—for the moment. The anger and other problems will resurface.

letting it OUT

Is it better to let your anger out in one huge explosion? Far from it. Explosions can cause you to:

INSULT OTHERS. People with anger problems may tease, taunt, or verbally abuse others.

HARM OTHERS. Some people let their angry emotions lead them to hit or hurt other people, even those who aren't to blame for making them angry. Others become violent to pets.

THROW TANTRUMS. Some people have total freak-outs when they're furious. They might scream, cry, swear, or stomp their feet. It's not a pretty sight when a teen has a temper tantrum.

DESTROY PROPERTY. Some people resort to breaking or smashing things, writing graffiti, or doing whatever damage they can to get rid of anger. This never solves the problem—and it can get you in trouble with the law.

TAKE REVENGE. Some people plot revenge schemes when they're angry at others, such as spreading nasty rumors or playing cruel pranks.

Passing It On

Then there are those kids who may not seem angry. But behind their smile, they may be seething.

Amy likes to say she doesn't get mad—she gets even. You'll never see her push someone in the hallway or yell at another girl during lunch. But you don't want to get on Amy's bad side. Just because Amy's anger is harder to spot than people's who throw things, it doesn't mean it's any less harmful.

If you were Amy's friend and she felt, say, that you ignored her at school, she just might forget to tell you that a bunch of kids are going to the mall on Saturday. When you found out, you'd be hurt. But Amy would swear it was just a big misunderstanding.

Then there was the time her mom told her to stay home and baby-sit her brother, when Amy really wanted to go over to a friend's house. She baby-sat, all right. But she let her brother eat a bag of cookies and watch R-rated movies on cable.

Amy's parents shake their heads, wondering what happens to her common sense. Her friends are equally perplexed. Is she really that forgetful? It sure doesn't seem like she means any harm.

Amy isn't forgetful. And she doesn't lack common sense. What neither her family nor her friends realizes is that Amy is very angry. But she doesn't show it in ways you might expect.

Amy exhibits a form of anger that psychologists call **passive-aggressive**. It's a hard one to

passive-
AGGRESSIVE

spot—even for the person who is angry. With this type of anger, people get back indirectly at those with whom they are angry. Passive-aggressive people may "accidentally on purpose" forget to do things for others. They may hand you a subtle insult disguised as a compliment. "My boyfriend is such a pain," they might say to a friend who wants a boyfriend. "You're so lucky you don't have one." In school, a passive-aggressive person may nod and smile at a teacher he's mad at and then skip class the next day.

Passive-aggressives are often people who are uncomfortable with anger. "They usually have backgrounds where all anger was considered a bad thing," says Dr. Louise Friendler. Many people who express anger this way have never learned how to show their feelings. "They can even convince themselves that they aren't really angry," she says. "After all, they aren't raising their voices."

PASSIVE-**AGGRESSIVE**

Some signs of passive-aggressive behavior are:

Being sneaky, like going out after curfew without telling parents or purposely going somewhere that is not allowed

Tending to sabotage things, such as parties or friends' plans

Often getting caught in lies

Saying one thing but doing another

Often blaming others

Rarely admitting mistakes

Tending to avoid direct conflict but often creating problems in other areas

Like other people, the passive-aggressive person has to learn how to be comfortable with his or her anger. Friendler teaches passive-aggressive teens to talk about how they feel. "A lot of times, they don't have the language for it," she says. "When you can get them to say, 'Yeah, that really made me mad,' that's a big breakthrough. They often have a hard time admitting that what they are really feeling is anger."

What Does Work?

Learning to change your behavior isn't easy. It may take time to learn a method that works for you and you'll need a lot of practice. According to the experts, there are three basic steps for managing anger that everyone should know about:

1 Do the Brain Work

Become more aware of your anger.

"If everyone around you is afraid of you, it's a good signal that your anger may be out of control," says Friendler. "If you can't see it, then you need to work on becoming more self-aware."

In a sense, being self-aware is admitting you have a problem. But it goes beyond that. It means recognizing your triggers and understanding the emotions that set you off. "Is it frustration? Is it feeling disconnected? Is it a feeling of worthlessness?" asks Dr. Bernard Golden. "It takes a lot of soul-searching to figure out why you are really mad."

Many people who have severe anger problems have very negative thoughts rattling inside their heads. To come to grips with your anger, you will have to look at the way you think.

Teach Your Body 2

After you've worked on your mind, you still have to deal with your body. The chemicals coursing through your brain can be difficult to control in the heat of the moment, and that's why things sometimes get out of hand. Experts say you should learn physical relaxation techniques, like deep breathing and muscle-relaxing exercises, to get back to a state where you can think clearly.

Golden recommends this exercise: Sit in a comfortable chair, close your eyes, and visualize a place that is extremely relaxing and peaceful. Imagine the colors, the sounds, the air quality. Then focus on how your muscles feel. Imagine your body becoming more relaxed—from your forehead to your face, jaw, neck, shoulders, and all the way down to your toes. Golden recommends practicing at least fifteen minutes a day.

With practice, your body learns to calm down on its own. You are training your body so it remembers how to react when you find yourself in a heated situation.

3 Develop Some Strategies

Relaxing your mind and body won't hold off all anger attacks.

At some point, someone will push your buttons. And you'll need to develop problem-solving skills that help you defuse a touchy situation.

"The ability to solve problems and communicate better with people is critical," Davis says. "You can't avoid every confrontation. But you can learn to work through them without letting your anger get out of control." You may need help developing your problem-solving skills. You can sit down with a parent or guardian, teacher, or health counselor. They can help you brainstorm ways of managing and communicating your anger.

But don't wait until you blow your stack to try out your new problem-solving skills. "This has to be developed [before you start to feel] really angry," Davis says. "When you are in the heat of your anger, it's too late to take a time-out and say, 'Hmm, how should I handle this?' You are too fired up to think clearly."

Other Strategies

There are many other creative and useful strategies for dealing with anger. Here are more strategies for dealing with anger in constructive and safe ways.

Role-Playing

Many anger management therapists say getting together with friends or family to role-play potentially hot scenarios can help you stay cool when you face problems in real life.

On the next three pages, you'll find descriptions of ten situations that could trigger anger or rage. With a partner, brainstorm possible responses to each of these situations. Think about which choices would be healthy ways to manage your emotions. Which choices would set you back? And be honest. Knowing which situations make you angriest is a great way to identify triggers.

TEMPER
tests

1. Someone at a party is flirting with your boyfriend or girlfriend. They are spending a lot of time talking to one another. You can't tell if your boyfriend or girlfriend is being polite or flirtatious, too.

2. Your mom wants you to mow the lawn. It's 100 degrees outside and you're playing video games in the air-conditioning. But she keeps calling you to go outside—now!

3. Your dad says you're not allowed to go to a concert. You've already told your friends you'll be there. You will be so embarrassed if you have to say you're not allowed to go.

4. You get your science project grade and it is lower than you think you deserve. You worked hard on your project. And you don't think the teacher gave you good instructions.

5. You come home and find your little brother in your room, going through your stuff. You've told him over and over not to go into your room if you're not there.

6. You think another student is spreading rumors about you.

7. You're online IM'ing your friends. Your mom comes in and tells you to shut off the computer until you finish your homework. You say "One more minute," but she insists you do it now.

8. Your parents are asking a lot of questions about your friends. They even want to talk to their parents. You start thinking, "Don't they trust me?"

9. You weren't invited to a friend's party. You thought the two of you were pretty close. You wonder if you did something wrong.

10. A kid bumps into you in the hallway. Your books drop. You whirl around. But he walks away like nothing happened.

Art Therapy

Art therapy has become a valuable tool in counseling. Whether it's drawing or sculpting, making art can help you work through problems like anger, depression, and grief. Advocates say it's particularly helpful for teens who are uncomfortable in talk therapy. "Art therapy is a nonthreatening, nonverbal path to discovery," says Deni Brancheau, a certified art therapist in Maryland. "It can help take what's going on inside and bring it out."

Robert, 17, has always been quiet and mild-mannered. When his grades slipped and he withdrew from his friends, his parents suggested he see a therapist.

> "Art therapy is a nonthreatening, nonverbal path to discovery."

Robert went along with the idea, mostly to avoid an argument. He was never comfortable talking about his feelings. But on the first day with his therapist, he instantly felt at home. Her office looked like an art studio, with everything from charcoal to paints to clay. Instead of asking Robert to tell her about himself, the first thing she did was hand him a blank piece of paper and ask him to draw anything he wanted.

"I was like, 'Well this is weird, but it's better than other doctors,'" says Robert. As he doodled, he barely realized that he was drawing a dark image: an overcast sky and what seemed to be a scene of downtrodden schoolkids being herded into a menacing-looking building. "I sat back and thought, wow, is that really how I feel inside?" he recalls. "It opened my eyes. I didn't know I was that angry about school."

Brancheau says she usually starts therapy with teens by giving them paper and asking them to draw whatever they feel. Often, she says, she's stunned by how quickly their art reveals what's troubling them. "The artwork is an extension of themselves," she says. "Engaging the person in the art process reveals what they are unconsciously struggling with."

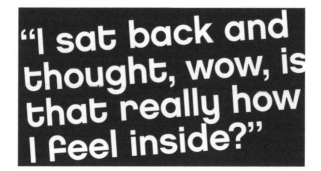

"I sat back and thought, wow, is that really how I feel inside?"

"I was always trying so hard to be a good student," Robert says. "I didn't know how much that was making me angry."

You can try art therapy at home. The American Art Therapy Association offers these do-it-yourself art therapy tips:

- Choose the medium that appeals to you. If you don't enjoy paints or clay, try colored pencils or chalk. You can also make collages with cut-up magazine pages.
- To loosen up, start by making sketches.
- Work quickly and intuitively, without planning or second-guessing.
- When you're done, examine your creation. Do any of the shapes or colors evoke feelings? Continue exploring these images to see if they evolve or become clear.

RELAXATION
TIME

Everyone unwinds in his or her own way. Here are some techniques for getting your mind off the things that are making you angry.

1 EXERCISE. Go for a walk or a run, work out, or play a sport. Exercise is a great way to improve your mood.

2 LISTEN TO MUSIC. Music can change a person's mood pretty quickly. Put on your headphones so you can play your music as loudly as you want without antagonizing anyone.

3 WRITE DOWN YOUR THOUGHTS AND EMOTIONS. You can write them in a journal or as poetry or song lyrics. After you've written them down, you can keep your writing or throw it away. Some people keep an anger diary, writing about each incident that makes them angry and how they handled it.

4 MEDITATE OR PRACTICE DEEP BREATHING. Find a quiet, comfortable place. With your eyes closed, focus on your breathing and the way your body feels. The more you do this, the more you'll learn to relax in stressful situations. Davis recommends repeating a mantra—or code word—that helps keep you calm. "You might just say, 'Calm' again and again as you take a deep soothing breath," he suggests.

5 TALK ABOUT YOUR FEELINGS WITH SOMEONE YOU TRUST. A good, sympathetic ear is always helpful, especially when dealing with the emotions behind your anger, such as sadness or rejection. Talk to a friend, a teacher, or a family member. One tip: Wait a little while before talking with the person you're mad at. You might need some distance before you can express yourself calmly. And Davis suggests staying away from e-mailing, text messaging, IM'ing, and posting on Web sites. "Once you put those things out there, you can't take them back after you've calmed down," he says.

6 DISTRACT YOURSELF. Get your mind off whatever you're mad about. Whether it's watching TV, playing a video game, reading, or going to the movies, do something that distracts you. Before you know it, you'll be too wrapped up in something else to even remember why you were so ticked off.

Anger Management Programs

N'Chelle is learning to avoid conflicts. But it's easier said than done. There are still girls at her school who get on her nerves. There are still times when she clenches her fist and wants to haul off and hit somebody. But when she feels that urge coming on, N'Chelle tries to step back. She takes a deep breath and counts to ten. The best thing, she finds, is simply to walk away.

After N'Chelle was suspended, she went to an after-school anger management program for teens. At first, she resisted. "I was like, 'These people say I've got a problem. Well, maybe they are the ones with the problem,'" she says. But as the weeks went by, she opened up to the other people and counselors in the program. "Talking really helped a lot," she says. "It was the first time I really could tell people what I was feeling."

Sometimes do-it-yourself strategies just aren't enough to deal with destructive anger. Anger management programs provide trained professionals to help and support you through the difficult process of understanding your anger. If you find that you are overwhelmed by anger and all the negative feelings that surround it, don't be afraid to seek help. Anger management counselors have seen every shade of anger and can guide you as you find your way.

LAUGH TRACK

Can HUMOR Help Soothe Your ANGER?

Everybody loves to laugh. But can humor really ease your anger? Studies show that laughter stimulates the immune system by increasing the number of natural antibodies. Laughter also lowers the level of serum cortisol, a substance released by the adrenal gland during stress. In addition, laughing exercises your lungs and increases the amount of oxygen in your blood.

But experts also note that not all humor is helpful when it comes to dealing with anger. "Silly humor or humor about yourself can be good," Davis notes. But harsh or sarcastic jokes can backfire. "The point is to take the person's mind off his anger and make him feel better," he says. "Putting him down with a cutting joke is going to have the opposite effect."

REST UP

A Good
Night's
Sleep Can
Chase
Your
Anger
Away.

Miss your beauty sleep, and you're probably awfully cranky the next day.

Different people require different amounts of sleep at night. But more than 47 million Americans don't get the minimum amount of sleep they need each night, notes the National Sleep Foundation (NSF). The organization believes there's a link between sleep deprivation and mood problems. An NSF survey shows:

People who get less than six hours of sleep on weekdays are more likely to describe themselves as stressed, sad, and angry.

People who report being sleepy during the day are likely to describe themselves as dissatisfied with life.

People who don't get enough sleep are more likely to get impatient or aggravated with common daily occurrences such as waiting in line or sitting in traffic.

acceptance and control

acceptance and control

"IT'S NOT LIKE YOU CARE!"

How Do You Handle Other People's Anger Without Igniting Your Own?

Your mom had a rough day at work. You were online when she came home, and she yelled at you to get off the computer and do your homework. Or read a book. Or get a job.

Your friend flunked her algebra test. You know she worked hard on it. So after class you stop at her locker. You start to say that the test was really tough. But she cuts you off. "It's not like you care!" she yells.

The kids at school have been making fun of your little brother. That night at dinner, he's in a terrible mood. Later, when you're watching TV, he grabs the remote out of your hand. When you tell him you had it first, he flings it at you, just missing your head.

Maybe you have your anger under control. You do your deep breathing. You know your triggers. And you've found a way to let off steam. But not everyone has come to terms with their anger. Wherever you go, you're going to run into someone who's angry. Maybe at the movies. Maybe at school. Maybe in your own house.

If you don't watch out, you can make the situation worse. Or their anger might trigger your own. In these cases, you'll need all of your anger management and communication skills. And you might need a few tips on how to deal with someone who's blown her stack.

Friendly Fire

What do you do if a friend loses his cool?

Try these tips:

- **Don't fuel the anger.** Try not to say or do anything that will make him madder. Get his mind off it instead. Talk to him about sports or TV or anything else.
- **Back off.** Sometimes when people are angry, they need time alone to cool off. Give them some space until they've chilled out a little.
- **Don't ignore bad behavior.** If your friend starts talking about hurting someone or venting his anger in destructive ways, get help. If you think your friend might hurt himself or others, talk to a teacher or parent immediately.

The I's Have It

No one thinks rationally when their temper explodes. And when trying to calm someone down, it's awfully easy to say the wrong thing. To find a constructive way to talk about your anger—or someone else's—you'll have to polish your communication skills. When talking to a friend about anger, you can often sound like you are accusing or attacking your friend, even if you don't mean to. You might say something like, "You're always picking on me for the clothes I wear—and you know I hate it!" You were trying to talk about how you felt. But instead, it turned into a blame game.

A great way to express yourself in these situations is through what anger experts call I-Statements. These are nonthreatening statements that say what you feel without blaming the other person.

An I-Statement has three parts. It goes something like this: I feel (fill in the blank) when you (fill in the blank) because (fill in the blank).

I FEEL (fill in the blank)
WHEN YOU (fill in the blank)
BECAUSE (fill in the blank).

Here's an example. Instead of saying, "You're always picking on me for the clothes I wear—and you know I hate it!" you can say, "I feel hurt when you make fun of my clothes because I really can't afford clothes that are more expensive."

Be specific about your emotions. And give details of how your friend has acted or what she has done to make you mad. The more clear and concise you are, the less you sound like you're blaming her. Instead of focusing on what she did, talk about how you feel. She'll get the message—and she won't feel like you're attacking her.

"I feel hurt when you make fun of my clothes because I really can't afford clothes that are more expensive."

Conflicting Reports

Anger is often caused by conflict. A disagreement between two people gets heated. Pretty soon harsh words are exchanged. Instant anger.

Okay, say you've learned how to manage your anger. Managing conflicts can still be difficult because you can't make other people manage *their* anger. But rather than scream and yell or get into a physical fight, there are ways of calmly solving the dispute. It's called conflict resolution.

What is conflict resolution? It can take many forms, but it usually means two people working out their differences in a calm and nonjudgmental atmosphere. Negative words and angry outbursts are checked at the door.

In many cases, conflict resolution involves a mediator, someone who's neutral and doesn't have loyalty to either side. A mediator listens to both sides of the argument and tries to come to a fair solution. There are even kid mediators at many schools who are good at helping other kids talk about their conflicts and work on solutions.

But you don't always need a mediator to resolve conflicts. All you need is a cool head and your anger management skills. In conflict resolution, it's important to clearly assert your side of the story—without blaming the other person. Then listen carefully to what the other person has to say. You might even be swayed by his argument!

DO-IT-YOURSELF
Conflict Resolution

You and your friend are feuding. Why not try Conflict Resolution, the Home Game! Just follow these six easy steps:

Step 1:

COOL OFF. Conflicts can't be solved in the face of hot emotions. Take a step back, breathe deeply, and get some emotional distance before trying to talk things out. Do something that makes you feel better when you're hot under the collar, like counting to 10 or splashing cold water on your face. When you've cooled down, you'll be ready to talk.

Step 2:

USE AN I-STATEMENT. It's a great tool for expressing how you feel without attacking or blaming. Avoid put-downs, guilt-trips, sarcasm, or negative body language. You need to be calm, fair, and willing to compromise.

Step 3:

REPEAT WHAT YOU HEARD. Each person tells their side of the story. Then you each repeat out loud what the other has said. Hearing the other person's point in your own words might help you understand the other perspective.

Finding Help

Do you ever feel unsafe due to a parent's rage? Are you in a relationship where anger has gone too far? Here are some resources to help you assess your situation and help you find a way to get help:

Prevent Child Abuse America
www.preventchildabuse.org
312-663-3520

The Rape, Abuse & Incest National Network
www.rainn.org
800-656-HOPE

National Domestic Violence/Abuse Hotline
800-799-SAFE

Childhelp USA
www.childhelpusa.org
800-4-A-CHILD

Teen Line
800-852-8336

Victims of Crime Resource Center
800-842-8467

Step 4:
TAKE RESPONSIBILITY. In most conflicts, both parties have some degree of responsibility. But we usually think that most—if not all—of the problem is the other person's fault. Be willing to take some blame—maybe even more than you think you deserve. When it's all over, you'll find that each of you shoulders some of the responsibility.

Step 5:
BRAINSTORM SOLUTIONS. There are many solutions to a single problem. Be creative. The key is a willingness to seek compromise.

Step 6:
FORGIVE AND FORGET. A handshake, hug, or kind word provides remarkable closure to a conflict. Just saying thank you or acknowledging the person for working things out sends a great message: This relationship can be saved!

Moving On

Even when we figure out exactly what's making us angry, we may not be able to fix it. A lot of things in life are beyond our control. When we get angry about these things, it can be especially hard to get past our mad feelings.

"In the end, there's a certain amount of powerlessness we sometimes just have to accept," says Dr. Louise Friendler. "Sometimes we work on our anger and we come up with great strategies, but there's still nothing we can do to change our circumstances. We just have to live with them."

Let's say your parents are moving, and you're going to have to leave your friends and start a new school. Or maybe your English teacher gave you a bad grade on a short story you worked really hard on because he just didn't like it. Or your car is stuck in traffic and you're going to be late for a friend's party.

No amount of problem solving is going to fix situations like these. Getting mad won't help. It will probably just make things worse. It's up to you to find ways to let go of angry feelings and accept that many things in the world are simply out of your hands.

think POSITIVE

What are some positive ways to express your anger? We asked teens what they do to cool off.

N'Chelle:

I'm a screamer, so sometimes I'll go outside when no one is around and yell really loud. If I feel like hitting something, I'll punch a pillow. It really works when you take a deep breath and count to 10. I like talking to people in my anger management group. I didn't think I would like it that much. But the people there really listen to me. And sometimes we can all laugh at the stupid things that get us mad.

Amy:

Music definitely helps me calm down. I like to put on my headphones and listen to my iPod. I close my eyes. It puts me in my own world.

Robert:

I'm drawing now when I feel angry or depressed. It's fun, and it takes your mind off things.

Paul:

I feel better when I'm really active. If I just sit down in one place, I'm going to start getting upset. I like to run laps. Or go to the gym and shoot baskets. I know someone who takes boxing lessons. He says it helps a lot to hit a punching bag.

Megan:

I've tried keeping a diary. Sometimes it's good. It's not like talking to a person. I can say anything I want in it. Other times, I'm too mad to sit down and do it. I like to go on the Internet and surf. After a while, I forget why I was mad. Sometimes I just take a nap. When you get really worked up, you can really crash!

adrenaline—a hormone secreted by the adrenal glands in response to stress

alienates—causes to be separate or unattached

amygdala (uh-MIG-duh-luh)—a section of the brain that is responsible for identifying threats

bipolar disorder—a psychological disorder characterized by extreme emotional highs and lows

catecholamines—chemical compounds that act as hormones or neurotransmitters, including dopamine and adrenaline

cortex—the outer layer of brain tissue that's involved in rational thought, voluntary movement, and the senses

depression—a psychological illness characterized by prolonged feelings of sadness

displaced anger—anger directed toward someone other than the person who caused the anger

fight-or-flight response—a physical response to a threat or stress that results in confrontation or flight

passive-aggressive—displaying behavior characterized by indirect resistance to others

perfectionism—a belief that anything less than perfect is unacceptable

prefrontal cortex—an area of the frontal lobe of the brain that plays a role in the regulation of emotions and behavior

rage—violent and uncontrolled anger

triggers—situations that set off a certain emotion or reaction

Books

Bohensky, Anita. *Anger Management Workbook for Kids and Teens*. New York: Growth Publishing, 2001.

Davis, Daniel. *Your Angry Child: A Guide for Parents*. New York: Haworth Press, 2004.

Eggert, Leona L. *Anger Management for Youth: Stemming Aggression and Violence*. Bloomington, IN: National Educational Service, 1994.

Golden, Bernard R. *Healthy Anger: How to Help Children and Teens Manage Their Anger*. New York: Oxford University Press, 2003.

Online Sites & Organizations

American Psychological Association
www.apa.org

The APA provides information and education about a variety of mental health issues for people of all ages. Check out the section "Controlling Anger—Before It Controls You." (www.apa.org/topics/controlanger.html)

Centers for Disease Control and Prevention
www.cdc.gov

The CDC is the top source for information on public health. Check out "BAM! Body and Mind," a section that provides teens with information about making healthy lifestyle choices. (www.bam.gov/sub_yourlife/yourlife_conflict.html)

86, 103
role-playing, 80

S
sabotage, 76
sarcasm, 63, 90, 100
screaming, 25, 28, 63, 72, 98, 103
self-awareness, 67, 77
serum cortisol, 90
sexual abuse, 34
sleep, 57, 71, 91
sneakiness, 76
sports, 12, 23–24, 66, 87, 95, 103
stomach aches, 29, 57, 62, 71
stress, 14, 19, 58, 88, 90, 91
suppression, 69–71

T
tantrums, 54, 72
taunting, 72
teasing, 72
Teen Line, 101
therapy, 84
triggers
  angry people as, 95
  embarrassment as, 81
  examples of, 81–83
  family responsibilities as, 14, 81, 82, 83
  friendships and, 17, 83
  frustration as, 12
  goals and, 9, 13
  hurt feelings as, 9, 12, 16
  identifying, 80
  loss as, 14
  perfectionism and, 14–15, 17
  recognizing, 29, 30–31, 67, 77

in relationships, 81
school as, 82, 83
siblings as, 16, 82
sleep and, 91
stress as, 12–13, 14

U
University of California, 10
University of Hawaii, 10
University of Pittsburgh, 58

V
verbal abuse, 72
Victims of Crime Resource Center, 101
violence, 26, 27, 28, 35, 36, 37, 72

W
warning signs, 28, 62, 63
weapons, 41
Web sites, 88, 101
withdrawing, 69
worthlessness, 69, 77
writing, 87, 103

About the Author

John DiConsiglio is a writer in the Washington, DC area. He is the author of several books for young people, including *Coming to America: Voices of Teenage Immigrants* (Scholastic, 2002) and *True Confessions: Real Stories About Drinking and Drugs* (Scholastic 2008). As a journalist, he has covered some of the top stories of the last two decades, from presidential elections to Supreme Court decisions to the tragedy at Columbine High School. His work has appeared in numerous magazines including *People*, *Glamour*, and *Cosmopolitan*. He is a graduate of Cornell University.